Montana Wildflowers

photography and text by
D. Linnell Blank

FARCOUNTRY PRESS

Dedicated to all who are working to protect wildflower habitat.

Acknowledgements

I am grateful for the help, patience, and sharing of expertise from my hiking companions, the Montana Native Plant Society members, the Glacier Camera club members, Tamara Blank and her family, Beverly Magley, Jim Mepham, Caroline Patterson, Dave Streeter, and Mom.

RIGHT: Western sweetvetch, *Hedysarum occidentale;* Sitka valerian, *Valeriana sitchensis;* arnica, *Arnica latifolia;* paintbrush, *Castilleja miniata;* near Inspiration Pass, Swan Range. The Swan Range has a brief but intense wildflower season in midsummer. (One of the most magnificent areas may be seen along Alpine Trail from Inspiration Point to Crevice Lake.)

TITLE PAGE: Blanketflower, *Gaillardia aristata,* mid-July, Garnet Range.

FRONT COVER: Bitterroot, *Lewisia rediviva,* beside the Missouri River at the foot of the Big Belt Mountains. The summer frost-free season is called the "growing season." Try telling that to the bitterroots. The leaves start growing during autumn rain and go dormant in the spring, which means the plant does all its growing during frost season.

BACK COVER: White pasque flower, *Pulsatilla occidentalis,* late June, Glacier National Park.

ISBN: 1-56037-368-7
Photography © 2005 by D. Linnell Blank
© 2005 Farcountry Press

For more information about our books write Farcountry Press, P.O. Box 5630, Helena, MT 59604; call (800) 821-3874; or visit www.farcountrypress.com.

Created, produced, and designed in the United States.
Printed in China.

09 08 07 06 05   1   2   3   4   5

Introduction
by D. Linnell Blank

Globeflower, *Trollius laxus*

Buttercup, *Ranunculus sp.*

Scarlet globemallow, *Sphaeralcea coccinea*

*C*olor attracts me to Montana wildflowers, from the intense ultramarine blue of a gentian to the delicate pastel of scarlet gaura. Other plants come in as spectacular an array of shapes and sizes, but only wildflowers will dazzle your eyes with a rainbow of intense hues. Looking for sparks of color to photograph lured me into searching out Montana's best blooms. When I come across a brilliant display of flowers, the camera gives me an excuse to linger. I approach carefully, trying not to crush any neighboring blossoms or make tracks that would detract from the scene. I look at the flower from different angles as I pore over the qualities that drew me to a particular patch. Was it the curve of the petals, the pattern of the stamens, or the sweep of meadow accented by wild colors?

By now, my knees are dirty, my nose is filled with rich scents, and I am enthralled with my subject. I know the morsel of it I am sharing with you cannot include the coolness of the air or the heady scents. But I hope these photographs can convey the excitement of these enchanting places.

Montana's flowering plants come in a wide range of sizes. The tiniest is the water-meal, *Wolffia columbiana,* or floating pond scum the size of a grain of sand and the smallest flowering plant in the world. The largest is the stately plains cottonwood tree, *Populus deltoids*—Montana's largest cottonwood is 108 feet tall and almost 13 feet in diameter.

These various groups of plant species thrive in neighborhoods called vegetation zones. Vegetation zones are determined by all the things that influence a plant's growth: the direction of a slope, elevation, growing season, rainfall, soil type, sunshine, temperature, and wind. The zones are helpful to know if you are hoping to find a particular wildflower, or if you are trying to identify a particular flower. I've grouped them into three vegetation zones in this book: alpine and subalpine, forests and foothills, and plains and valleys. Even so, most species are found in more than one zone, so use these as a rough guide.

You can get a vivid display of Montana's vegetation zones

by getting to a viewpoint overlooking mountains and a broad valley or prairie. Near Big Timber, for example, you can see the rocky, treeless summits of the Crazy Mountains, their timbered slopes, and the grassy valleys and prairie at their feet. This horizontal band of trees between the foot and the tops of mountains characterize many of Montana's mountain ranges.

Most of Montana's wildflowers are well adapted to fire. Fire exposes the forest floor to the sun and cuts down on the competition from trees, and the ashes give the soil a burst of mineral nutrients. Snowbrush ceanothus and Bicknell's cranesbill, in fact, depend on fire to scarify their seeds so they can germinate. After the fire they sprout, taking advantage of the blackened soil that warms more quickly.

How do you find wildflowers? The easy answer: Look in the area where you spotted them last year. Most of Montana's wildflowers are perennials, so the plants will come up year after year. But you have to time it just right. Though a few wildflowers are bold enough to bloom in March, the most colorful time for most of Montana's wild-flowers is from mid-May through July. Look for scarlet globemallows, yuccas, and prickly pears on the prairies, shooting stars and camas in the valleys, and arrowleaf balsamroots, lupines, and biscuitroot in the foothills. In September, you may still find a few late-blooming harebells and asters covered in frost.

What if you missed the show last year? Good places to look for blooms are unplowed and relatively undisturbed stretches of land. Pastures can be great if they are not too heavily overgrazed. Conditions vary on public lands, but they are good places to look because they are open to the public. Check out the numerous state and national parks, national forests, wilderness areas, and Bureau of Land Management lands. For a sheer profusion of flowers, try the Pryor Mountains, the Gravelly Range, the Beartooth

Plateau, the Rocky Mountain Front, the unforested parts of Glacier National Park, and the Swan Mountains.

You will find more flowers and notice more about their surroundings if you travel on foot. There is something about hiking up a steep slope that gives nearly everyone a sudden breathless interest in the details of small plants!

It is great fun to learn to identify wildflowers. It is not necessary to learn their names. Just start recognizing the friends that come visiting once a year. Soon, you may recognize their leaves. Then something won-derful happens. One early spring or late summer, you will be strid-ing across a green hill, and when you look down, you'll realize that what you are walking through is not grass, but leaves. The leaves of your old friends. You will

Sticky geranium, *Geranium viscosissimum*

realize that you are actually walking through a field of wild-flowers—it's just that they are sleeping.

There are many places I have been in Montana where nearly every living thing I see can bear a beautiful blossom, even if they are not blooming at the moment. When I know this, I can visualize the confetti of colors and intoxicating scents of the blooming flowers, even if the leaves beneath my feet are just greening up after a long winter's sleep.

Alpine and Subalpine

Montana's alpine zone is located in the 25 mountain ranges in west, central, and southern Montana where summits are high enough to get summer freezes, which prevents trees from growing and leaves the terrain wide open for wildflowers. This zone is characterized by deep cold, intense sunshine, drying winds, rocky landscapes, and huge views.

In areas level enough to accumulate soil, you will see many of the same wildflower species that you see in the subalpine zone. The windy, rocky slopes are dotted with the charming mat-forming and cushion plants. They are tiny plants with full-sized blooms. White-flowered alpine dryads, pink stars of moss campion, and Jones columbine, whose deep lavender-blue blossoms sprout from limestone talus, snuggle in close to the ground to avoid the chilling and drying effects of the wind. Alpine fireweed's blossoms are similar in size to common fireweed, but the plant is 4 to 16 inches tall instead of 4 to 7 feet.

Below the treeline, which varies in elevation from 7,500 to 9,300 feet in Montana, only three tree species—Engelmann's spruce, subalpine fir, and whitebark pine—can handle the short growing season, heavy snow pack, and cold, moist, conditions. These trees define the subalpine zone. While it is a tough place for trees, wildflowers love it! The short growing season forces many species to bloom at the same time, resulting in a multi-hued carpet of large, showy wildflowers, including the yellow daisy-shaped arnica and groundsel, the hot-pink-tipped splitleaf paintbrush, the lacy bridal whites of Sitka valerian, and beargrass, a member of the lily family that is the showiest plant of the subalpine zone.

LEFT: Glacier lily, *Erythronium grandiflorum,* and globeflower, *Trollius laxus,* Pitamakan Lake, Glacier National Park. The snow had just retreated from the shores of Pitamakan Lake, and glacier lilies and globeflowers were already in full bloom. How did they do it? The sprouting plants absorbed sunlight that penetrated the heavy spring corn snow; this heat melted small holes in the ice around the flowers so they could emerge. Many plants depend on a good snow pack to survive the winter.

7

TOP: Western sweetvetch, *Hedysarum occidentale,* and fleabane, *Erigeron* sp., White River Pass, Bob Marshall Wilderness.

ABOVE: Alpine clover, *Trifolium dasyphyllum,* near Wyoming Creek, Beartooth Plateau.

LEFT: Alpine fireweed, *Chamerion latifolium,* near Boulder Pass, Glacier. Sun shining through the smoke of a wildfire casts warm light on alpine fireweed. South of here, I was kneeling, quietly photographing fireweed on another smoky evening, when I looked up and saw a grizzly running straight toward me at full speed, with two cubs behind her. Between us, a ground squirrel screamed and dove for its hole. After I retreated a few hundred yards, talking in a "calm" voice, she resumed her hunt for ground squirrels, dashing back and forth among the boulders and fireweed.

TOP RIGHT: Paintbrush, *Castilleja rhexifolia*, Logan Pass, Glacier.

BOTTOM RIGHT: Thistle, *Cirsium* sp., Vipond Park, Pioneer Mountains.

FAR RIGHT: Paintbrush, *Castilleja rhexifolia*, Mary Baker Lake, Floral Park, Glacier. Floral Park is a fabulous place to see flowers growing on terrain given up by Sperry Glacier and its predecessors. You will need to hike about 20 miles, half of that off-trail, so there isn't much time to stop and smell the roses.

TOP AND FAR RIGHT: Alpine spirea, *Spiraea densiflora,* and beargrass, *Xerophyllum tenax,* Mount Grinnell, Glacier. People often think beargrass blooms every seven years. Not so. The plump underground stems form offshoots that become the next generation of flowers. Once the parent plant blooms and sets seed, it dies back to its base. This cycle tends to take five to seven years, but is not like clockwork.

BOTTOM RIGHT: Lupine, *Lupinus* sp., near Pintler Pass, Anaconda Pintler Wilderness.

TOP: Rosecrown, *Sedum roseum,* and saxifrage, *Saxifraga occidentalis,* near Cracker Lake, Glacier.

ABOVE: Spotted saxifrage, *Saxifraga bronchialis,* Highline Trail, Glacier. A casual look at spotted saxifrage reveals succulent leaves packed so close they resemble moss and flowers only a quarter inch across. Look closely at the flowers and you will see they have tiny spots.

LEFT: Cushion buckwheat, *Eriogonum ovalifolium,* near Triple Divide Pass, Glacier.

TOP RIGHT: Forget-me-nots, *Boraginaceae,* near Wyoming Creek, Beartooth Plateau. The yellow or white centers of forget-me-nots are nectar guides or signposts for arriving pollinators, showing them where to go to find pollen-rich stamens. Using paper cutouts of forget-me-nots, scientists found that without nectar guides, bees spent too much time walking around the flower to adequately feed themselves.

BOTTOM RIGHT: Sticky Jacob's-ladder, *Polemonium viscosum,* on the Beartooth Plateau near Line Creek Plateau.

FAR RIGHT: Penstemon, *Penstemon ellipticus,* at Crevice Lake, Swan Range. The rocky ledges below Thunderbolt Mountain hold lakes with intricate shapes, niches for wildflowers, and views into the Bob Marshall Wilderness.

TOP AND LEFT: White mule's ears, *Wyethia helianthoides,* near Mill Creek, Tobacco Root Mountains. If you look closely, you will see the blossom center is made up of dozens of tiny yellow flowers. Each is a separate flower, and, in fact, each of the white "petals" is a distinct flower, too! This arrangement is typical of the plants in the enormously diverse family called Asteraceae, like asters, sunflowers, and daisies.

ABOVE: Thread-leaved sandwort, *Arenaria capillaris,* near Inspiration Pass, Swan Mountains.

TOP: Round-leaved violet, *Viola orbiculata,* on the trail to Granite Peak, Glacier.

ABOVE: White marsh marigold, *Caltha leptosepala,* Branham Lakes, Tobacco Root Mountains.

LEFT: Lewis monkeyflower, *Mimulus lewisii;* arnica, *Arnica* sp.; and groundsel, *Senecio* sp.; below Mount Oberlin, Glacier. The moist meadows here consistently put on a huge wildflower extravaganza in July.

TOP: Explorers bog gentian, *Gentiana calycosa,* near Indian Springs, Bob Marshall Wilderness.

ABOVE: Yellow columbine, *Aquilegia flavescens,* on the Highline Trail, Glacier.

LEFT: Fleabane, *Erigeron* sp.; paintbrush, *Castilleja miniata;* Sitka valerian, *Valeriana sitchensis;* western sweetvetch, *Hedysarum occidentale;* near Inspiration Pass, Swan Range. I was hiking with friends and they said they smelled a bear—the smell was worse than a wet dog. Years later, I learned that that smell in subalpine terrain after an end-of-summer frost comes from wilting Sitka valerian.

TOP: Sticky Jacob's-ladder, *Polemonium viscosum,* Firebrand Pass Trail, Glacier.

ABOVE: Harebell, *Campanula rotundifolia,* on a log jutting into Lace Lake, Mission Mountains.

RIGHT: Fleabane, *Erigeron peregrinus,* and Lewis monkeyflower, *Mimulus lewisii,* above Hole-in-the-Wall, Glacier. If you are eager to see less-wide-ranging wildflowers, find water. Carnivorous plants prefer wet places: butterworts, for example, thrive on dripping ledges and sundew plants prefer swamps and bogs. Fringed grass of parnassus are found by streams and seeps. Yellow mountain-avens, in river gravels. Wet meadows are good places to look for irises, blue camas, and shooting stars. Monkeyflowers grow near streams, sometimes directly in the spray of a waterfall.

TOP LEFT: Eightpetal mountain-avens, *Dryas octopetala,* on the north shoulder of Flinsch Peak, Glacier.

BOTTOM LEFT: Ross's avens, *Geum rossii,* on the Beartooth Plateau near Line Creek Plateau.

FAR LEFT: Cinquefoil, *Potentilla* sp., Vipond Park, Pioneer Mountains. Vipond Park has broad open meadows full of cinquefoil and camas. In the chiseled white granite of the Pioneer Mountains, you can also see regional endemics, plants that are found only in a limited area, including the Lemhi penstemon, *Penstemon lemhiensis,* whose royal-blue blooms are found in only four counties in Montana and one in Idaho.

TOP: Elephanthead, *Pedicularis groenlandica,* near Oreamnos Lake, Anaconda-Pintler Wilderness.

ABOVE: Silky phacelia, *Phacelia sericea,* Lubec Ridge, Badger–Two Medicine.

RIGHT: Blanketflower, *Gaillardia aristata,* and sticky geranium, *Geranium viscosissimum,* on the slopes below Altyn Peak, Glacier, with Mount Wilbur in the background. The south-facing slope of Altyn Peak has an assortment of wildflowers but also spotted knapweed, which came from Europe. Spotted knapweed, a noxious weed, has been aggressively taking over, crowding out other plants.

Forest and Foothills

*P*lants in the forest receive moderate moisture and cool temperatures, but they have to compete with other plants for sunlight, moisture, and soil nutrients. Many understory forest plants have broad, deep-green leaves that gather as much light as possible in the dappled shade. Flowers tend to be scattered and shy. Some, such as woodnymph and pipsissewa, even nod to face the ground.

The forest is full of complex relationships. Take calypso orchids, for example, one of 20 species of orchids in Montana's forests. Each orchid has one leaf, which grows in autumn and withers away in spring, but the plant is nourished by fungus called mycorrhiza, that grows in the soil around trees. You will never find a calypso orchid far from a conifer and its mycorrhiza.

Foothills get more moisture than the valley floor—about 15 to 25 inches of precipitation per year—and support open grasslands and groves of aspen, Douglas fir, Rocky Mountain juniper, and ponderosa and limber pines. The hills, gullies, ridges, and rocks provide microhabitats that support different assortments of plants. The pasqueflower is one of the earliest-blooming foothills flowers. The showiest is probably the arrowleaf balsamroot with its oversized yellow daisy heads and giant fuzzy leaves.

LEFT: Arnica, *Arnica* sp.; Lupine, *Lupinus* sp.; and sticky geranium, *Geranium viscosissimum*; on the west side of the Crazy Mountains. After wading through a field of sticky geranium to take photos, my hands and pant legs were sticky, too! Botanists conjecture that the stickiness of our grassland plants may be a defense against bugs, almost serving as fly paper. Montana has several species of true carnivorous plants that have bladder traps or sticky traps to catch and digest insects to supply important nutrients.

TOP: Clematis, *Clematis occidentalis*, Lubec Ridge, Badger–Two Medicine.

ABOVE AND LEFT: Pasqueflower, *Pulsatilla patens*, Lubec Ridge. The pasqueflower is a good example of what happens when plants are transported abroad to similar climates and don't encounter the microbes and bugs that plague them at home. This beautiful Montana native is a troublesome weed in Australia. Tall coneflower, Canada goldenrod, Washington lupine, and plains cottonwood are other Montana natives that have run amok on other continents.

ABOVE AND FACING PAGE: Bitterroot, *Lewisia rediviva,* beside the Missouri River at the foot of the Big Belt Mountains. Bitterroot is called *Lewisia rediviva* because early botanists had a difficult time trying to preserve the plant for study. On his return trip in 1806, Meriwether Lewis dug up a plant and carefully labeled, pressed, and dried it. A year and 3,000 miles later, he presented it to botanists in Philadelphia. When they examined it, the bitterroot had begun to sprout! The name *"Lewisia"* is in honor of Captain Lewis and *"rediviva"* means "restored to life."

TOP: Lance-leaved stonecrop, *Sedum lanceolatum*, Looking Glass Pass, west of Browning

ABOVE AND RIGHT: Arrowleaf balsamroot, *Balsamorhiza sagittata,* Gold Butte, Sweet Grass Hills. The three buttes of the Sweet Grass Hills rise up from the prairie to scrape extra moisture from the passing clouds. This moisture supports abundant wildlife and a variety of plants, including these arrowleaf balsamroot, *Balsamorhiza sagittata,* which sprouts from a taproot that can grow up to 4 inches in diameter and 8 feet long. The sense of limitlessness and beauty in the Sweet Grass Hills make it easy to understand why several American Indian tribes view this land as sacred.

TOP RIGHT: Claspleaf twisted-stalk, *Streptopus amplexifolius,* Fern Creek, Glacier.

BOTTOM AND FAR RIGHT: Trillium, *Trillium ovatum,* and western red cedar, *Thuja plicata,* Ross Creek in the Scotchman Peaks, the Cabinet Mountains. These plants are the same species that grow in the drizzly climate near the coast of Washington state. Several valleys of northwestern Montana catch so much moisture wafting in from the Pacific Ocean that they foster temperate rain forests.

ABOVE: Douglasia, *Douglasia montana,* and draba, *Draba* sp., Lubec Ridge, Badger–Two Medicine.

FACING PAGE: Douglasia, *Douglasia montana,* and wolf lichen, *Letharia vulpina,* Lubec Ridge. My favorite place for the first wildflower hike of the season is Lubec Ridge in the third week of May. If spring has been mild, there will be arrowleaf balsamroot, silky phacelias, death camas, paintbrushes, serviceberries, and lupines. If the spring was cold, you will likely see these early bloomers: douglasias, drabas, glacier lilies, kittentails, pasqueflowers, shooting stars and yellowbells. The Badger–Two Medicine is a wedge of terrific wildlife habitat between Glacier and the Bob Marshall Wilderness, so bring your binoculars. You can see elk and grizzlies, sometimes even bison!

TOP RIGHT: Wild hollyhock, *Iliamna rivularis,* by St. Mary Lake, Glacier.

BOTTOM RIGHT: Fairy slipper, *Calypso bulbosa,* Columbia Mountain Trail, Swan Range. The fairy slipper exploits the inexperience of newly hatched bees in order to achieve pollination. Lured by the flower's yellow bristles that it thinks contains nectar or pollen, the bee enters the flower. Pollen sticks to the bee's back, where the bee can't reach it. There is no nectar. But, because each blossom has a different pattern of spots, the bee will try another calypso orchid. As it enters the flower, the pollen on its back touches the even stickier female part of the second flower, and pollination is achieved. Eventually the bee avoids Calypsos, but another naive young bee will take its place.

FAR RIGHT: Blanketflower, *Gaillardia aristata,* and lupine, *Lupinus* sp., Many Glacier Valley, Glacier.

ABOVE: Paintbrush, *Castilleja hispida,* Lubec Ridge, Badger–Two Medicine. Paintbrushes are hemiparasites, which means they produce some of their food with their own green leaves, but the rest is filched from their neighbors. Within their first weeks of life, the paintbrushes grow finger-like projections that attach themselves to other plant roots, from which they start sucking water and nutrients. Near Red Lodge, for example, nearly every Wyoming Indian paintbrush, *Castilleja linariaefolia,* is cuddled in next to a sage bush.

FACING PAGE: Paintbrush, *Castilleja hispida,* Little Chief Mountain, Glacier.

45

TOP LEFT: Glacier lilies, *Erythronium grandiflorum,* near Two Medicine, Blackfeet Indian Reservation.

BOTTOM LEFT: Mountain lady's slipper, *Cypripedium montanum,* near Fish Creek, Glacier.

FAR LEFT: Glacier lilies, *Erythronium grandiflorum,* below Goat Mountain, Glacier. When I see a fantastic abundance of glacier lilies, I pinch off a stem and flower and pop it into my mouth for a wonderful combination of sweet and peppery flavors.

TOP: Fuzzytongue penstemon, *Penstemon eriantherus,* mid-July, Garnet Range. Penstemons are showy flowers in an actively evolving genus. There are 30 different species in Montana, and some of them hybridize with each other and create chaos for taxonomists, whose challenging job it is to classify living things.

ABOVE: Short-styled onion, *Allium brevistylum,* near Mill Creek, Tobacco Root Mountains.

LEFT: Cow parsnip, *Heracleum sphondylium,* and fireweed, *Chamerion angustifolium,* in the St. Mary Valley, Glacier.

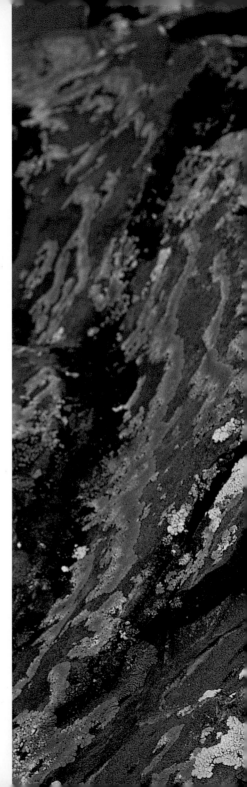

TOP: Pointed mariposa, *Calochortus apiculatus,* near Anaconda Creek, Glacier. These mariposas bloomed prolifically in the aftermath of the 1999 Anaconda Creek wildfire. Lilies store their energy in underground bulbs that are safe from a fire's heat and allow the plant to pop out of the ground in the spring, when the lilies take advantage of the flush of nutrients and reduced competition in the fire's wake.

ABOVE: Parry's Townsendia, *Townsendia parryi,* Tobacco Root Mountains.

RIGHT: Draba, *Draba* sp.; lichens; and Parry's Townsendia, *Townsendia parryi;* near Ear Mountain, Rocky Mountain Front.

TOP LEFT: Sego lily, *Calochortus nuttallii,* in the Meeteetse Spires at the foot of the Beartooth Mountains.

BOTTOM LEFT: Blue bead lily, *Clintonia uniflora,* the Danny On Trail, Whitefish Range.

FAR LEFT: Shrubby cinquefoil, *Pentaphylloides fruticosa,* near Blindhorse Creek, Rocky Mountain Front. The Rocky Mountain Front, which stretches 100 miles from Glacier to Rogers Pass, is where the mountains meet the prairies. It has dramatic displays of wildflowers. The extravaganza starts around the third week of May with swaths of shooting stars in low damp flats, pasqueflowers on the hills, and douglasia on the rocks. In late May and June comes the cacophony of balsamroot, camas, lupines, paintbrushes, potentillas, serviceberries, sticky geraniums, and vetches. If there are spring and summer rains, wildflowers can last well into July.

Plains and Valleys

Many of us know that the terrain above the treeline is considered alpine. But southern, southwestern, and central Montana also have a low timberline, below which it is too dry for trees to grow. In areas that receive around 10 to 16 inches of precipitation, even our most drought-tolerant timber, the Ponderosa pine, gets too thirsty and gives up. The elevation of the lower timberline varies greatly—it is between 2,300 feet in the Missouri Breaks to 7,500 feet in the high dry valleys of southwest Montana.

This leaves most of eastern and central Montana open for the short-grass prairie, which is the open country known as Big Sky Country. In northwestern Montana, the valleys are moist enough to be forested. The dry, intermountain valleys are dominated by bunchgrasses and the Palouse prairie flora also found in northwest Idaho and eastern Washington.

Though you may find swaths of prickly pears or a slope punctuated with huge spikes of yucca blossoms, prairie wildflowers are usually found hiding in the grass. Special niches such as moist gullies may feature fire-work-bursts of bergamots or depressions full of elegant wild irises. Rain-water pouring off the side of a road can supply three times more water than neighboring plants get, which results in parades of sunflowers, scarlet globemallows, and evening primroses lining the byways. Around rocks, the shallow soils give wildflowers a break from competition with grasses, so these rough-looking locations may be some of the most colorful, sprouting with yellow balls of cushion buckwheat and bright pink pea-blossoms, or plump fuzzy buds of rabbitfoot crazyweed.

RIGHT: Scarlet globemallow, *Sphaeralcea coccinea,* on an eroding bank of the Judith River. These tough prairie plants, also known as cowboy's delight, don't seem to mind drought and overgrazing. The plant must have evolved to tolerate the grazing of pronghorns, bison, and prairie dogs. At times, the showiest wildflowers are growing from the pile of dirt at a ground squirrel's hole.

TOP: Shooting star, *Dodecatheon* sp., near Two Medicine, Blackfeet Indian Reservation.

ABOVE: Wild bergamot, *Monarda fistulosa,* on the Meeteetse Trail at the foot of the Beartooth Mountains. If you roll the stems of this plant in your fingers, you will feel that it is square in cross-section. This, along with the aromatic scent, is a characteristic of the mint family. Use these characteristics to identify other Montana mints, such as field mint, *Mentha arvensis,* or self-heal, *Prunella vulgaris.*

LEFT: Shooting stars, *Dodecatheon* sp., meadow below the Livingston Range, Glacier.

TOP: Asteraceae, early June, near the Judith River.

ABOVE: Sego lily, *Calochortus nuttallii,* in the Terry badlands along the Missouri River, northeast of Miles City.

LEFT: Asteraceae, late May, Milk River and Rookery Wildlife Management Area. Just west of Havre, the Rookery Wildlife Management Area has native flowers, fossils, sculpted badlands, and bright red hills made of scoria or clinker. The clinker is a layer of sediment baked hard like brick when the coal seam beneath it caught fire and burned. This process is responsible for many colorful rugged hills in eastern Montana.

TOP RIGHT: Rocky Mountains iris, *Iris missouriensis,* late June, East Pryor Mountains.

BOTTOM AND FAR RIGHT: Plains pricklypear, *Opuntia polyacantha,* and threadleaf phacelia, *Phacelia linearis,* on the banks of the Judith River. A one-foot-wide clump of prickly pear may have roots reaching out two or three feet that can utilize as little as one-tenth of an inch of rain. Prickly pear flowers open rapidly. One warm morning, as I was photographing a partially opened prickly pear bud, I noticed that my composition had changed. While I was engrossed, the flower had fully opened!

TOP: Silky lupine, *Lupinus sericeus,* near Rock Creek, near Red Lodge.

ABOVE: Phlox, *Phlox* sp., Gold Butte, Sweet Grass Hills.

LEFT: Lupine, *Lupinus* sp., sunrise, Crazy Mountains. For photographers, sunrise and sunset are "the magic hour" because the soft twilight and the low-angled golden beams are rendered particularly well on film. How inconvenient! To catch the sunrise, I set my alarm and groan when it goes off. But a while later, I am watching the Milky Way fade into a rainbow of sunrise colors. The wind drops, lakes become mirrors, the flowers halt their incessant dance and hold still for photos, and the first beams light the peaks with alpenglow.

TOP AND FAR RIGHT: Yucca, *Yucca glauca,* at the foot of the Pryor Mountains. Yucca blossoms are designed for one admirer only, the yucca moth, *Tegeticula yuccasella,* the only creature that can pollinate the white blooms. The yucca moth, oddly enough, can eat only one thing—yucca seeds!

BOTTOM RIGHT: White penstemon, *Penstemon albidus,* near the Judith River.

TOP LEFT: Goldenpea, *Thermopsis montana,* along Mill Creek, Tobacco Root Mountains.

BOTTOM LEFT: Skunk cabbage, *Lysichiton americanus,* LeBeau Research Natural Area, Salish Mountains. The humbling thing about wildflowers is that this festival of scent, color, and shape is not meant for us. It's for insects, like bees and butterflies, that perform the important job of carrying the male pollen from one flower to the female stigma of another. This becomes clear when you get a whiff of skunk cabbage. That smell is certainly not created for attracting us, but it attracts this plant's chosen pollinators—flies.

FAR LEFT: Goldenpea, *Thermopsis rhombifolia,* Suction Creek, Bears Paw Mountains.

TOP: Plains pricklypear, *Opuntia polyacantha,* west of Twin Bridges.

ABOVE: Dryad, *Dryas drummondii,* west fork of the Teton River, Rocky Mountain Front.

RIGHT: Plains pricklypear, *Opuntia polyacantha,* the eastern side of the Pryor Mountains. The Pryor Mountains put on a big wildflower show in late spring and early summer. At high elevations, each broad hillside is tinted with a different hue. Desert shrubs, sagebrush, and wildflowers of Bighorn Canyon dot the mountain's eastern edge (see page 74). The Pryor Mountains also have limestone parapets and walls, caves, wild horses, and an expansive view that takes in a lot of southern Montana and northern Wyoming.

TOP LEFT: Blue camas, *Camassia quamash,* Christensen Meadows, Glacier.

BOTTOM LEFT: Rocky Mountain beeplant, *Cleome serrulata,* west of Twin Bridges.

FAR LEFT: Blue camas, *Camassia quamash,* and larkspur, *Delphinium bicolor,* below the Nevada hills. Blue camas is a wildflower that has started a war. Its bulbs were such an important food source to the Native Americans that the digging grounds were fought over in the Bannock War of 1878. Blue camas can bloom so profusely that from a distance it looks like a lake.

TOP RIGHT: Blue flax, *Linum lewisii,* near Canyon Creek, Pioneer Mountains.

BOTTOM RIGHT: Clustered broomrape, *Orobanche fasciculata,* near Sage Creek, Pryor Mountains. The diminutive clustered broomrape is tucked in next to a variety of larger plants. Like paintbrushes, broomrapes have specialized roots for drawing water and nutrients from other plants. But unlike paintbrushes, it is completely parasitic. Its copious seeds, some of the tiniest in the plant kingdom, filter down through cracks in the soil to germinate near the roots of a host plant.

FAR RIGHT: Blue flax, *Linum lewisii,* early July, Ruby Valley.

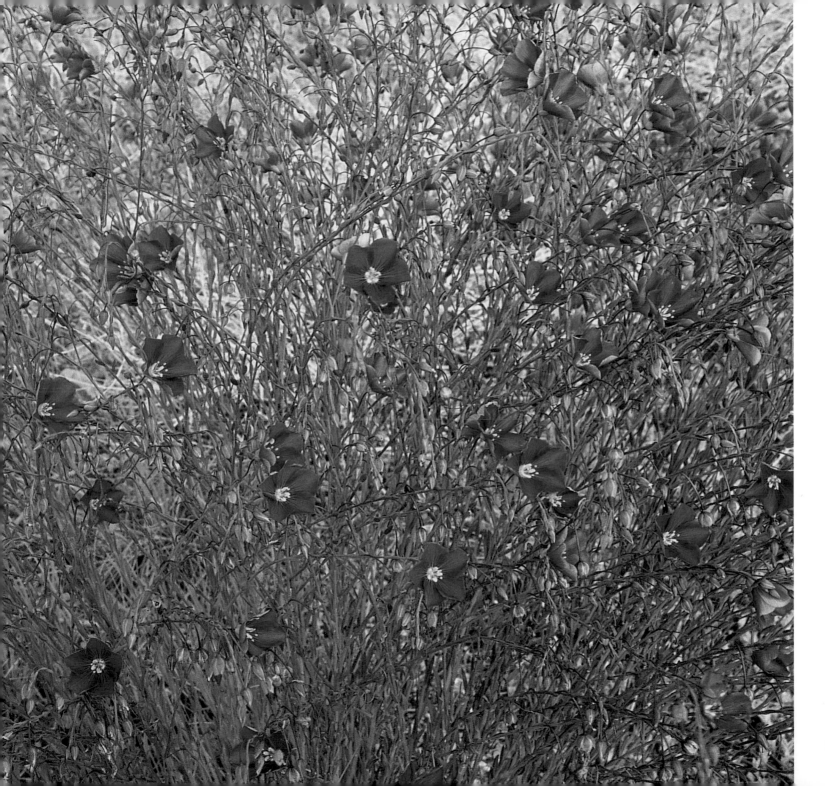

TOP LEFT: Downy paintedcup, *Castilleja sessiliflora,* near the White Cliffs, Missouri River.

BOTTOM LEFT: Tufted evening-primrose, *Oenothera caespitosa,* in Lime Kiln Gulch near Wise River. The blossoms open in the late afternoon, a pristine white. The next morning they are drooping and have darkened to pink after enduring a wild night of insect reproduction.

FAR LEFT: *Asteraceae* and *Fabaceae,* Bighorn Canyon, north of Trail Creek. Bighorn Canyon, which seems as if it belongs in Utah or Arizona, has fantastically sculpted rock—some of it a deep red—and, with less than six inches of rain annually, is the hottest, driest terrain in Montana. Yet it has beautiful wildflowers, including masses of prickly pear blossoms and yucca.

TOP: Yellow fritillary, *Fritillaria pudica*, Lubec Ridge, Badger–Two Medicine.

ABOVE: Prairie smoke, *Geum triflorum*, by the North Fork of the Flathead River. Look closely at wildflowers such as prairie smoke and it can be shocking to see how hairy they are. Why are they so unshaven? The hair provides a little shade from the strong sunlight and ultraviolet radiation. It also slows down the breeze on the surface of the plant, which preserves the plant's moisture. When the weather is cool, it traps heat and lets the plant continue its many chemical processes. The hairiest flowers live on the prairie, foothills, or alpine slopes where conditions are harshest.

RIGHT: Lupine, *Lupinus* sp., and shrubby cinquefoil, *Pentaphylloides fruticosa*, below Choteau Mountain on the Rocky Mountain Front.

TOP: Hairy false goldenaster, *Heterotheca villosa,* mid-July, near Red Lodge.

ABOVE AND LEFT: Ovalleaf buckwheat, *Eriogonum ovalifolium,* and McCartney Mountain, west of Twin Bridges. This highly variable and attractive plant is treasured by rock gardeners. Prospectors called it "silver plant" because they thought it showed the location of silver. Certain plants are "indicator plants" because they indicate the presence of minerals like nickel, zinc, or selenium, or gauge how acidic, alkaline, or salty the ground is.

D. Linnell Blank

I always said I didn't want to try photography because it would be expensive and habit-forming. Then in 1988, I needed a slide of one of my small pen and ink drawings and my rangefinder couldn't focus close enough. I bought a 35-millimeter single-lens reflex camera and was captivated. Photography felt like sculpture, carving out what was unnecessary, emphasizing what was there. And my hunch was right: it was habit-forming.

I grew up in New York and Massachusetts and graduated from Middlebury College in 1979. Since moving to Montana in 1985, I have hiked and back-packed in many parts of the state from the Cabinet Mountains to Makoshika State Park, learning about wildflowers.

My first published photograph appeared in

Whitefish Magazine in 1991. My work has been exhibited at Artistic Touch Gallery and at the Hockaday Museum of Art, and, since 1999, has frequently appeared in *Montana Magazine,* including the covers of the 2002 calendar and the January 2005 magazine.

Getting to know wildflowers helped me know Montana on a deeper level. The blossoms tell me about weather, soils, climates, and how the nuances of conditions—such as a change in slope angle—can make a huge difference to living things. And flowers that burst forth in a blaze of glory for a few weeks and spend the rest of the year waiting underground, only to do it again, have taught me about loving a place and suffering with it through tough times, and then, when conditions are right, springing up to spread joy and beauty to others.